WRITTEN BY
SAM SEDGMAN

ILLUSTRATED BY
DANIEL LONG

EPIC CITIES

FOR MY BROTHER, ALWAYS
BUILDING SOMETHING—SAM SEDGMAN

FOR M & D, FOR ALWAYS SUPPLYING PENCILS,
PAPER, AND ENCOURAGEMENT—DANIEL LONG

KINGFISHER
LONDON & NEW YORK

Text copyright © Sam Sedgman 2025
Illustration copyright © Macmillan Publishers International Ltd 2025
First published 2025 in the United States by Kingfisher,
120 Broadway, New York, NY 10271
Kingfisher is an imprint of
Macmillan Children's Books, London
All rights reserved

Distributed in the U.S. and Canada by Macmillan,
120 Broadway, New York, NY 10271

Library of Congress Cataloging-in-Publication Data has been applied for.

ISBN 978-0-7534-7936-0

Kingfisher books are available for special promotions and premiums.
For details contact: Special Markets Department, Macmillan,
120 Broadway, New York, NY 10271

For more information, please visit
www.kingfisherbooks.com

Printed in China
1 3 5 7 9 8 6 4 2
1TR/1124/UG/WKT/128MA

Senior designer: Jim Green
Senior editor: Catherine Saunders

EU representative: 1st Floor, The Liffey Trust Centre,
117-126 Sheriff Street Upper, Dublin 1 D01 YC43

MIX
Paper | Supporting
responsible forestry
FSC® C116313
FSC
www.fsc.org

EPIC CITIES

WRITTEN BY
SAM SEDGMAN

ILLUSTRATED BY
DANIEL LONG

KINGFISHER
LONDON & NEW YORK

A WORLD OF CITIES

Half of the world's people live in cities. Nestled among mountains, sprawled in desert flats, or perched at the mouths of rivers, cities have sprung into life all over our planet. Each one is different. Some were carved from ancient stone by powerful empires, while others shoot up into the sky with glittering towers of metal and glass. Some huddle from icy winds on rocky coastlines, others swelter in tropical heat. From the food people eat to the way they travel, from weather to industry to religion— every city is as wild and varied as the land it's built on and to the people who call it home.

Cities are bursting with life!

Under the skin of every city is a hive of activity. Gushing pipes, aqueducts, and reservoirs fetch water for thirsty mouths, gardens, factories, and fountains. Roaring power plants send electricity surging through pylons to light up skyscrapers, billboards, stadiums, and cinemas. Streets hum with the rumble of metro trains, the purr of buses, and the bells of bicycles. And everywhere, there are people —chattering in cafes, playing soccer in the park, or slurping noodles in nighttime markets.

When so many people live together, they have to become clever about how they shape their streets. There are always questions to answer: Where does the water come from? Is the air clean? Where will people go to work, to learn, and to have fun? How can they cope with traffic, with a heatwave, or with a natural disaster? Every city answers these questions differently and so every city lives in a different way.

Each city has adapted to its own unique issues in its own way. In *Epic Cities*, you'll discover how Montreal deals with thirteen million tons of snow every year, how Cape Town scares off wild baboons, how Venice is built on water, and how Reykjavík can harness the power of an erupting volcano.

This book will take you around the world and show you some of the most marvelous cities on Earth. On each page you'll see how a city has tackled a particular challenge in a unique and fascinating way. From the cable cars of Medellín to the recycling plants of Stockholm, from the Tokyo metro to the markets of Marrakesh, these cities have used smart thinking, clever design, and epic engineering to become extraordinary places to live.

Along the way, you'll see slices of everyday life in these incredible places, discovering more about each city's customs, favorite foods, activities, and even the animals who live there. There are also a few extra pages, crammed with even more facts about how cities around the world thrive and survive.

So grab your backpack, your compass, and your metro card. The world's most incredible cities are waiting for you to discover them, and there's something spectacular to find in every neighborhood.

Let's start exploring!

Sam Sedgman

CONTENTS

NORTH AMERICA

REYKJAVÍK

MONTREAL

MIAMI

MEDELLÍN

SOUTH AMERICA

RIO

EUROPE

STOCKHOLM

COPENHAGEN

LONDON   ROTTERDAM

KRAKÓW

PARIS

BARCELONA   VENICE

ISTANBUL

ATHENS

MARRAKESH

AFRICA

MECCA

ASIA

BEIJING

SEOUL

TOKYO

MUMBAI

SINGAPORE

AUSTRALIA

CAPE TOWN

MELBOURNE

A steel and glass "climate ribbon" at Miami's outdoor shopping mall, Brickell City Centre, provides shade and encourages cooling breezes to reduce heat without air conditioning.

In 2023, Miami had 46 days in a row above 100°F (37°C).

Heatwaves are now being named, like storms are, to help people become aware of how serious they are.

KEEPING COOL

Older buildings in hot countries are designed to keep cool. Outside, white paint reflects the sun and porches give shade. Inside, high ceilings let hot air rise, and windows on two sides create a breeze, with shutters blocking sunlight while letting air pass.

Modern air conditioning sucks heat from the air to keep buildings cooler inside. But this takes lots of energy, and makes the outside air even hotter.

Miami's basketball team is called the Miami Heat.

Miami's architecture is full of Latin American influences, thanks to many people moving to the city from Cuba, Puerto Rico, and South America.

Almost 70% of Miamians speak Spanish at home.

Miami has the world's first "chief heat officer" to help the city deal with extreme temperatures. The officer encourages people to check on their neighbors during heatwaves.

HEAT IN MIAMI

Glittering in the Florida sun, the beachfront city of Miami is no stranger to heat. As climate change makes extreme weather more common, excruciating heatwaves are causing deadly harm to cities around the world. Miami, one of the hottest cities in the United States, is using a variety of creative measures to safely cool itself down.

FEELING THE HEAT

Many things in cities make heat, including vehicles, stoves, factories, and computers. Hard surfaces such as bricks and concrete can absorb this heat, trapping it in the city.

MIAMI

Vehicle exhaust creates heat. Better public transportation and shady places to walk help fewer people choose to drive, which makes the city cooler.

Getting too hot can make us very sick, through dehydration, fainting, or heatstroke. It can even be deadly—extreme heat kills 30 people in Miami every year.

Trees create shade, absorb heat, and manage moisture in the air. Miami aims to cover 30% of its streets with a canopy of trees by 2030.

Miami's "cool pavements" are coated in a special paint to reflect heat back into the sky.

Water fountains help people stay hydrated on hot days.

Cooling centers in Miami's libraries and parks provide shelter from the heat.

Manatees live in the waters along Miami's coast.

THE EIXAMPLE

Until the 1850s, Barcelona was surrounded by fortress walls and was very overcrowded. When the walls came down, Barcelona could expand, and the "Eixample" district was built. "Eixample" means "expansion" in Catalan.

Cerdà's blocks intended rich and poor to mix together, with useful buildings such as markets, schools, and hospitals spread evenly throughout the district.

The Eixample was architect Ildefons Cerdà's vision of a perfect city. He thought carefully about what each citizen needed to live happily there, even calculating how much air each resident needed.

The Sagrada Familia is Gaudí's most famous work. This enormous church has been under construction for more than a hundred years. Gaudí is buried in its crypt.

Spanish architect Antoni Gaudí designed many iconic buildings in Barcelona. His designs were inspired by nature and are full of color, texture, and curving lines.

Few of Cerdà's ideas were kept. Blocks became taller and denser, and their inner spaces were built over. But the neighborhood remains a success and an icon of modern Spanish design.

DESIGN IN BARCELONA

All cities are planned in some way, but none show the touch of an architect's hand more than Barcelona. Famous today for its human-made beach and the fantastical structures of designer Antoni Gaudí, this thriving Spanish port is also dominated by a grid system called the Eixample (expansion), which was the biggest piece of urban design of its time.

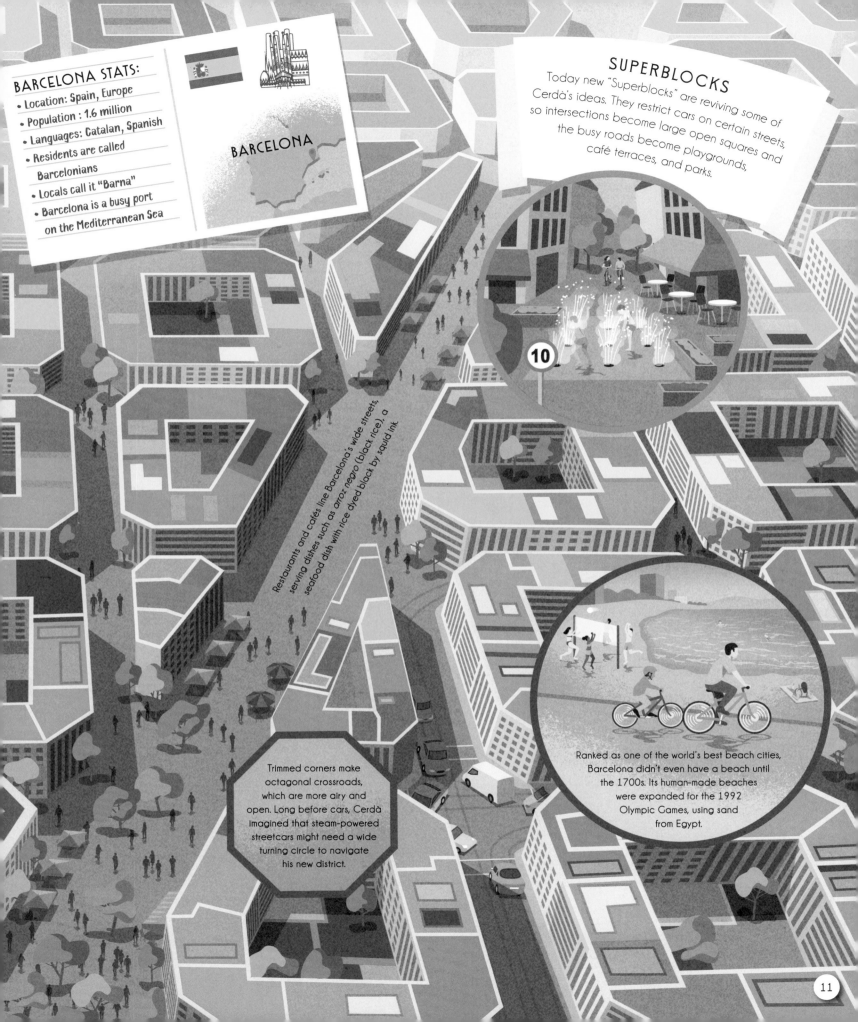

BARCELONA STATS:
- Location: Spain, Europe
- Population: 1.6 million
- Languages: Catalan, Spanish
- Residents are called Barcelonians
- Locals call it "Barna"
- Barcelona is a busy port on the Mediterranean Sea

SUPERBLOCKS
Today new "Superblocks" are reviving some of Cerdà's ideas. They restrict cars on certain streets, so intersections become large open squares and the busy roads become playgrounds, café terraces, and parks.

Restaurants and cafés line Barcelona's wide streets, serving dishes such as arroz negro (black rice), a seafood dish with rice dyed black by squid ink.

10

Trimmed corners make octagonal crossroads, which are more airy and open. Long before cars, Cerdà imagined that steam-powered streetcars might need a wide turning circle to navigate his new district.

Ranked as one of the world's best beach cities, Barcelona didn't even have a beach until the 1700s. Its human-made beaches were expanded for the 1992 Olympic Games, using sand from Egypt.

THE METRO IN TOKYO

プラットホーム1

Many large cities use underground rail systems, often known as the metro or subway, to help people travel around quickly and efficiently. At almost 100 years old, Tokyo's metro isn't the oldest or the largest, but it is the busiest: around nine million people travel on its 13 lines, 243 stations, and 2,700 trains every day.

SHINJUKU STATION

Shinjuku station is the busiest in the world, serving 3.6 million passengers every day. It has 200 exits, 51 platforms, its own map, and a bus to take you from one side to the other.

In Japan, almost 8.5 million tons of seafood is eaten a year.

Helpful diagrams show which train car is best to board with luggage, or to be closest to the exit at your destination.

Arrows on the floor show people where to walk, and everyone follows them.

Some Metro platforms have five-minute restaurants where commuters eat standing up. It's thought to be very rude to eat on the train.

Shibuya

Lines are coded by colors and letters, and each station has a number to help travelers who can't read Japanese.

Passengers are usually silent—it's considered disrespectful to talk on the metro.

The seats on the metro are heated.

09:18:32

Trains arrive sooner than every two minutes during rush hour and are punctual to the second.

Stations play calming bird noises and nature sounds to help passengers relax.

CROWD CONTROL
Four billion riders use the metro each year. Even when it's busy, it's orderly. People line up at marked points for the first, second, or third train.

Trains get so busy during rush hour that staff called "pushers" help squeeze everyone into the car.

Almost all lost items are handed in. Even a 100 yen coin, worth less than $1, was handed in and given its own lost-and-found report. Almost 20% of all lost items are umbrellas.

Stations are cleaned around the clock. There aren't many trash cans, so people take their garbage with them.

TOKYO STATS:
- Location: Japan, Asia
- Population: 14 million
- Language: Japanese
- Residents are called Tokyoites
- 45 of the world's 50 busiest train stations are in Tokyo
- Tokyo has the busiest metro system in the world

TOKYO

It's not uncommon to see tired people asleep on the metro.

DELIVERIES IN LONDON

Moving letters and packages quickly through heavy traffic has always been a struggle for busy cities, including London. Lying abandoned beneath its twisting, narrow streets, the "Mail Rail" system used to carry millions of letters a day, showing the ingenuity required to keep information moving through one of the busiest cities in the world.

Around 250,000 pigeons were used to deliver information during World War II. 32 of them were awarded medals.

London's first postal service began in the 1600s, but for royals' and officials' use only. Later anyone could send mail, but the recipient had to pay for it, which proved awkward.

Written information is now mainly sent by email instead of by letter. More than 347 billion emails are sent worldwide every day.

Around three billion packages are sent each year in the U.K.

Today hundreds of bicycle couriers speed through London's traffic to deliver vital documents and packages.

The Royal Mail delivers about seven billion letters a year, down from a height of around 17 billion in the 1990s.

VOTES FOR WOMEN

In 1909, two suffragettes sent themselves to the prime minister using the Royal Mail's same-day delivery service. However, the official at 10 Downing Street refused to sign for them.

Delivering the right mail to the right people is serious business. It's illegal to open someone else's mail.

MAIL RAIL

Mail Rail was an automated narrow-gauge railroad 6.5 ft. (20 m) beneath London's streets. Around 22 mi. (35 km) of track linked eight platforms beneath busy Royal Mail sorting offices and train stations. This system moved letters and packages quickly through the city.

Mail Rail opened in 1927, cutting travel time across the city from several hours to 30 minutes.

Mail Rail ran for up to 22 hours a day.

Live animals could once be sent through the mail, as long as they were "larger than a bee, and smaller than an elephant."

At its peak, Mail Rail carried four million letters a day.

Trains were driverless and electric, traveling at up to 30 mph (50km/h) between stations—almost three times faster than the traffic above.

Post was sorted by hand on mainline trains bringing mail to London.

During World War II, the mail tunnels were used to house important artifacts from the National Portrait Gallery and the British Museum. Here they were protected from any bombing.

Mail Rail was closed in 2003, as the declining volume of letters and the increased cost of running the old system made it too expensive. Part of it remains open as a museum.

LONDON STATS:
- Location: United Kingdom, Europe
- Population: 9 million
- Language: English
- Residents are called Londoners
- Nickname is "The Big Smoke"
- Over 400 million packages are delivered here every year

LONDON

15

CAFÉS IN MELBOURNE

Public places to eat and drink have long shaped the characters of the world's cities, giving people somewhere to meet, talk, and be seen. With its streets packed with independent cafés and restaurants, modern Melbourne has become a global center for food lovers, and the world capital of coffee culture. It shows how a thriving street scene can help cities feel alive.

Cafés have been associated with community, creativity, and social change since European cities discovered coffee in the 1600s. Leading artists and thinkers would meet in cafés, and their conversations might spark ideas for novels, inventions, or revolutions.

Someone who makes coffee is called a "barista" (the Italian word for bartender).

CAFÉ CULTURE

World War II brought Italian and Greek immigrants to Australia. They re-created their relaxed European café culture and introduced the espresso coffee machine to Melbourne.

There are over 2,000 cafés in Melbourne. Many of them are independently owned.

TASTE MAKERS

Melbourne's restaurant scene draws food lovers from around the world. "Pop-up" restaurants in unusual spots such as parking lots and old factories let chefs show off their new food ideas.

Vegetarian sushi

Mushroom fudge

Beef tongue

Kangaroo tails

Plum sodas

Honey and salt croissants

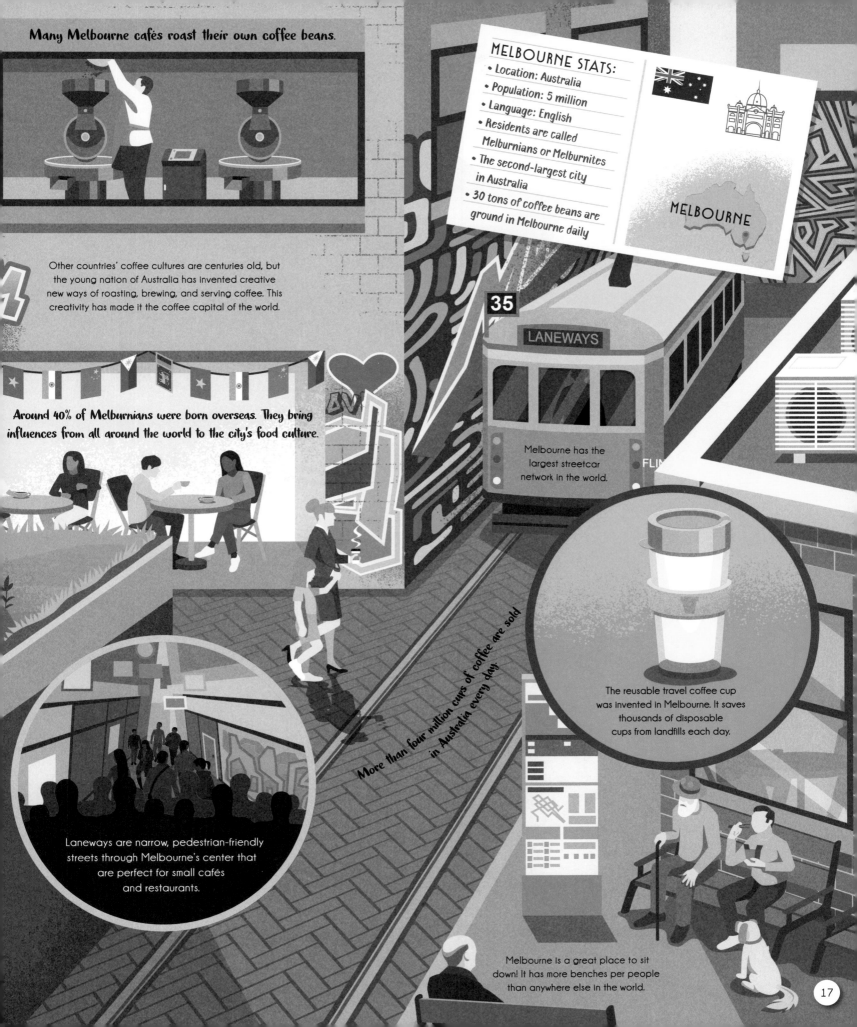

Many Melbourne cafés roast their own coffee beans.

MELBOURNE STATS:
- Location: Australia
- Population: 5 million
- Language: English
- Residents are called Melburnians or Melburnites
- The second-largest city in Australia
- 30 tons of coffee beans are ground in Melbourne daily

MELBOURNE

Other countries' coffee cultures are centuries old, but the young nation of Australia has invented creative new ways of roasting, brewing, and serving coffee. This creativity has made it the coffee capital of the world.

Around 40% of Melburnians were born overseas. They bring influences from all around the world to the city's food culture.

35 LANEWAYS

FLIN

Melbourne has the largest streetcar network in the world.

More than four million cups of coffee are sold in Australia every day.

The reusable travel coffee cup was invented in Melbourne. It saves thousands of disposable cups from landfills each day.

Laneways are narrow, pedestrian-friendly streets through Melbourne's center that are perfect for small cafés and restaurants.

Melbourne is a great place to sit down! It has more benches per people than anywhere else in the world.

FESTIVALS

Cities are always full of life! Now and then, they erupt into spectacles of joy and color, as people come together to celebrate. From ancient religious festivals to brand-new traditions, a city's calendar is peppered with special moments to honor its art, animals, food, famous residents, and more. Some are wild and wacky, others more serious and sincere. Here are some of the most unique and exciting festivals from around the world.

HOT-AIR BALLOON FESTIVAL
Albuquerque, New Mexico, United States

Over 500 hot-air balloons lift off from the city of Albuquerque each October, filling the skies with color and unusual shapes. The largest gathering of its kind, the festival draws aeronauts from around the world, who take part in "rodeo" races of speed and skill. The event finishes with a nighttime carnival with fireworks.

MONKEY BUFFET FESTIVAL
Lopburi, Thailand

A lavish feast is laid out in the ruins of the Phra Prang Sam Yot temple each November, to be eaten by the thousands of monkeys who live there. These animals are treated with respect and seen as a sign of good luck, and honoring them is a tradition that goes back 2,000 years. Dancers in monkey costumes kick-start the festivities and draw the animals' attention to their buffet, where more than three tons of fruit, vegetables, and sweet treats are displayed for them in towers and on huge platters.

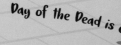

Day of the Dead is celebrated all over Central and South America.

DAY OF THE DEAD
Mexico City, Mexico

Día de los Muertos (Day of the Dead) sees friends and families gather to remember their loved ones who have died. Throughout Mexico's largest city, visits are made to candlelit graveyards, and families leave gifts at homemade altars, throw elaborate feasts, and decorate the city with colorful skulls.

WATER GUN FESTIVAL
Seoul, South Korea

Seoulites cool off from the summer heat by taking part in an enormous water fight. More than 100,000 people take to the streets and drench each other with water pistols. First launched in 2013, the festival has expanded into a gigantic water-themed party, with a parade, live music, bubble machines, aquatic obstacle courses, and even fire trucks taking part to spray cool water over the crowds.

WORLD AIR GUITAR CHAMPIONSHIP
Oulu, Finland

Experts at playing imaginary instruments gather in Finland each year to win the title of best air guitar performer. A panel of judges decides which of the international contestants plays their invisible instrument the best, and the winner is awarded with . . . a real guitar.

WORLD BODY-PAINTING FESTIVAL
Klagenfurt, Austria

Artists show off their creativity with stunning designs in the world's largest body-painting festival. A wild spectacle of ink and color, the festival transform's one of Klagenfurt's parks into "Bodypaint City" and attracts tens of thousands of visitors. A week of workshops let artists share their expertise, and a string of prizes are given out in a variety of contests, including a "makeup battle."

HENLEY-ON-TODD REGATTA
Alice Springs, Australia

A boat race held more than 600 mi. (1,000 km) from the nearest body of water, this quirky Australian tradition began as a mockery of the posh regattas held by the British colonizers. "Boats" are carried by teams through the hot sand of the dry Todd River, cheered on by a large audience. In 1993 it was canceled because of bad weather . . . rain meant there was water in the river!

RECYCLING IN STOCKHOLM

In forward-thinking Stockholm, garbage is seen as a resource, not a burden. Pledging to create zero new waste by 2029, the Swedish capital has an elegant system to recycle its trash into new materials, with everyone from children to big corporations taking part.

RECYCLED BY DESIGN

In Sweden, whoever makes an object is responsible for how it's disposed of. Companies must consider how to make things recyclable, instead of leaving recycling up to ordinary people.

Sweden aims to be "zero waste," meaning that everything is recycled.

Shoppers in Stockholm get money back for returning used bottles and cans to special recycling points. About 90% of items are recycled this way.

STOCKHOLM STATS:
- Location: Sweden, Europe
- Population: 1 million
- Language: Swedish
- Residents are called Stockholmers
- Known as "Beauty on the Water"

STOCKHOLM

klädaffär

You can be fined 800 Kronor, (about $75), if caught littering.

Unwanted clothes can be taken to stores, which shred them into fibers that are then spun into new clothes.

Children are taught how to recycle in school, and they take part in a national litter-picking day.

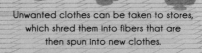

RECYCLING AT HOME

In Stockholm, household waste has to be carefully separated into many different categories: newspapers, cardboard, colored glass, metal and cans, clear glass, plastics, food waste, and "combustibles"—things that can be burned, such as diapers and paper towels.

Sweden makes money and energy by importing other countries' waste and recycling it for them.

Each type of waste is sorted into its own container, ready for recycling.

Every year, Stockholmers recycle about 1,000 lb. (450 kg) each—that's the same weight as a grand piano.

Food waste and sewage are turned into biogas, which fuels Stockholm's buses.

Combustible garbage is burned in local power plants to make energy. The leftover ashes are used to make roads.

Residents put separated waste into different collection tubes.

Stockholm is built over 14 islands, linked by more than 50 bridges. With pollution low, the water is clean enough to fish from and swim in.

Underground pipes transport waste to the recycling center at 45 mph (70 km/h) using compressed air. This means there are fewer garbage trucks that contribute to traffic, noise, and smell.

THE CAPE DOCTOR

Flat like a table, Table Mountain rises 3,563 ft. (1,086 m) above Cape Town. A hot dry wind usually covers the peak in a thin white cloud, like a tablecloth. Known as the "Cape Doctor," this breeze clears the air of smog and pollution.

Cape Town's mountain ridge is a natural habitat for baboons, but the city's expansion has forced them closer to humans.

BABOONS IN CAPE TOWN

Perched on Africa's southwestern tip, picturesque Cape Town boasts a treasure trove of wildlife. However, as the growing city has intruded on the natural habitat of local baboons, chaotic clashes have emerged. Cape Town's "Urban Baboon Programme" defuses conflict and tries to help people and baboons coexist safely.

Some of the baboons have GPS collars to help scientists understand their behavior.

Baboons live in social groups called "troops," which are led by an alpha male.

POWERFUL PRIMATES

Baboons are extremely intelligent monkeys that are native to Africa. Cape Town's are the largest type: chacma baboons, which can grow up to 5 ft. (1.5 m) tall and weigh up to 90 lb. (40 kg). Their sharp noses can sniff out food from 2 mi. (3 km) away.

Baboons' bottoms are covered in thick, cushion-like skin, which helps them sit upright on tree branches.

CAPE TOWN STATS:

- Location: South Africa, Africa
- Population: 4.6 million
- Languages: Afrikaans, Xhosa, English
- Residents are called Capetonians
- Cape Town is the southernmost city in Africa

CAPE TOWN

BABOONS VS. HUMANS

Baboon numbers grew after humans hunted local leopards, a key predator, to extinction. Now baboons can cause chaos in the city as they hunt for food, finding human food tastier than their natural diet. South African baboons were vegetarians until the 1800s, when they raided local farms and developed a taste for meat.

Baboons can climb walls and open doors, and they aren't scared of humans.

Residents can call a 24-hour baboon hotline to report problems.

City rangers act like a rival troop to try and persuade baboons off human turf.

Baboons are a protected species and can't be hunted as pests.

ROWDY RESIDENTS

Cape Town is home to more than 100 unique animal species, some of whom also cause problems for humans. A sanctuary was set up for thousands of penguins after they dug up local gardens.

Migrating flamingos attract birdwatchers to Cape Town.

Fur seals often sunbathe at the waterfront.

23

THE DEAD IN PARIS

Underneath Paris is a maze of old mines where millions of human bones are kept. It's a grim but ingenious solution to a problem every city faces: where to put its citizens when they die. Above ground, modern monuments and cemeteries honor brilliant philosophers and artists who have made Paris famous, keeping the city's legacy alive.

Most of Paris is built from limestone, which was dug from the mines beneath it. New buildings can't be more than a certain height or weight, in case they collapse into the tunnels below—that's why there are so few skyscrapers here.

GRAVE DANGER

In the 1700s, Paris's graveyards were overcrowded and smelly, causing dangerous disease outbreaks. To solve the problem, the old cemeteries were closed, their bones were moved into abandoned mines in nighttime funeral processions, and new graveyards were opened at the edge of the city.

Paris's largest cemetery, Père Lachaise, is the most visited in the world. Many of the one million graves here belong to famous artists and writers.

Citizens honored in the Pantheon include chemist Marie Curie and entertainer and activist Josephine Baker.

The Pantheon is an enormous former church where the remains of important French citizens are laid to rest.

Parisian cafés are famous for their fine food and lively atmosphere.

There are hidden entrances to the mines all over the city—in church crypts, beneath manhole covers, through forgotten doors in metro stations, and more.

CAFÉ de PA

METRO

THE CATACOMBS

The bones of six million people were transferred from Paris's graveyards into a 1.25 mi. (2 km) section of the old mines, named "the Catacombs." Today the whole network of mines is often referred to as the Catacombs.

After being largely forgotten for over a hundred years, the Catacombs were rediscovered in the 19th century and became a tourist attraction.

People who explore the catacombs for fun are called "Cataphiles." Some organize parties and art exhibitions.

ARRÊTE!
C'EST ICI L'EMPIRE DE LA MORT

A sign at the Catacombs' entrance reads: "Stop! This is the empire of Death."

The tunnels stretch over 185 mi. (300 km.)

A small part of the Catacombs has become a museum, but exploring the rest of the mines is illegal. However, many illicit explorers, called "Cataphiles," do explore the mines. The dark maze of tunnels is dangerous—if you got lost, you might never find your way out.

During World War II, the French Resistance kept their headquarters in the tunnels, where they plotted to take back the city from the Nazis.

Police once found a fully-working cinema abandoned in a cave in the Catacombs.

PARIS STATS:
- **Location:** France, Europe
- **Population:** 2.1 million
- **Language:** French
- **Residents are called** Parisians
- **Known as the "City of Lights"**
- **Built above** 185 mi. (300 km) of old mining tunnels

PARIS

DABBAWALAS IN MUMBAI

Every day, more than 200,000 home-cooked meals are packed into lunch boxes and delivered to the desks of workers and students across Mumbai. They're carried by dabbawalas—special couriers who weave through the chaos and traffic of the world's busiest city. Despite using no technology, they're always on time and almost never make a mistake.

The idea started in 1890, when a hungry banker wanted a home-cooked lunch, so he paid someone to go and fetch it from his house and deliver it to his office.

HOME-COOKED MEALS

Most meals are cooked outside the city by family or staff. The food is packed into special tiffin tins, which keep it hot and separated in compartments.

ON THE TRAIN

At around 10:30 a.m., after the morning rush hour, the lunch boxes are taken to local stations to be sorted onto trains. Mumbai has the busiest train network in the world, carrying more than two billion passengers a year.

India's first train was in Mumbai, along with its first bus and first airport.

Lunch box lids are painted with color-coded letters and numbers, which explain where the box comes from, where it's going, and who is delivering it.

At the station, dabbas are sorted by destination and put into crates for each train.

Lunches are collected at around 9 a.m. Meals have to be ready on time—dabbawalas have a schedule to keep!

"Dabba" means lunch box. "Dabbawala" means "one who carries a lunch box."

MUMBAI CENTRAL
मुंबई सेंट्रल

Dabbawalas often have only 30 seconds to board the train with their sorted lunch boxes, so everything has to be perfectly organized.

THE RACE IS ON

Every lunch box needs to be delivered by 1 p.m. Each weighs about 4.5 lb. (2 kg), and dabbawalas carry up to 35 a day. They use expert knowledge of the city's short cuts to avoid traffic and make their deliveries on time. Mistakes are made in less than one in 3.4 million deliveries.

LUNCHTIME

Lunches are delivered between 12 p.m. and 1 p.m. Dabbawalas deliver six days a week—a six-day workweek is common in much of India.

A typical lunch might include vegetable curry (sabji), lentil dal, rice, salad, pickles, and roti flatbread.

Everyone respects the importance of the dabbawalas' task, and people often give way to them.

Mumbai is the home of Indian cinema, known as "Bollywood."

बॉलीवुड फिल्म

दुकान

चाय

कपड़े की दुका

कैफे.

After lunch, dabbawalas collect the lunch boxes and return them home, using the same system in reverse.

The dabbawala network has been studied by big tech and delivery companies, who admire its efficiency.

MUMBAI STATS:

- Location: India, Asia
- Population: 21 million
- Languages: Marathi (official), Hindi, English, Gujarati
- Residents are called Mumbaikars
- Mumbai is the most densely populated city in the world
- Mumbai is not the capital of India; New Delhi is.

MUMBAI

WATERWAYS IN VENICE

Venice is built on a cluster of islands in a marshy lagoon on the edge of the Adriatic Sea. This "floating city" has no roads, so people use canals, boats, and bridges to get around. Today rising tides and sinking buildings mean that city planners must find creative ways to help this beautiful city stay above the water.

The water in the lagoon is brackish—a mix of salt water and fresh water.

GETTING AROUND
Venetians travel by foot, or by boat along the 25 mi. (41 km) of canals. There are no cars, and even bicycles and skateboards aren't allowed.

Public transportation in Venice is by "vaporetto," a boat bus.

BUILDING THE CITY
The lagoon's many islands were reinforced with bricks to support buildings. The waterways in between became the canals.

Gondolas are small black rowboats that ferry passengers around the city, like taxis. They are icons of Venice!

It's illegal to swim in Venice's canals.

Gondolas are 36 ft. (11 m) long. They are slightly crooked, which makes it easier to row with one oar.

Over 400 bridges cross Venice's waterways. Many are private, such as the famous Bridge of Sighs.

Venice is prone to floods. When high tides surge in from the Adriatic Sea, 78 floodgates rise up from the lagoon floor to block the water. They sink back down again to let ships pass.

VENICE STATS:
- Location: Italy, Europe
- Population: 260,000
- Language: Italian
- Residents are called Venetians
- Known as "Serenissima" ("the most serene")
- Venice consists of 118 small islands

VENICE

One of the world's narrowest streets is in Venice: it's only 21 in. (53 cm) wide.

The Grand Canal's speed limit is 3 mph, but emergency vehicles go much faster.

Venice's largest waterway is the Grand Canal. It's 2.5 mi. (4 km) long, 16 ft. (5 m) deep, and runs through the heart of the city.

Millions of wooden poles support Venice's buildings. Each of them is about 16–40 ft. (5–12 m) long.

THE SINKING CITY
Venice sinks every year by about 0.04 in. (1mm), as its heavy buildings compress the silty islands they are built on.

Venetians eat a lot of seafood. Moleche are small green crabs that are fried and eaten whole—including the shell!

Many rules protect Venice's streets. Picnics are outlawed, and no one is allowed to feed the pigeons.

LOST CITIES

Across the world, ancient and modern civilizations have left behind relics of urban life, which can become ghostly windows into another time. These eerie, empty places may have been the victims of disaster, suffered from a change of power, or simply become the shadow of a way of life whose time has passed.

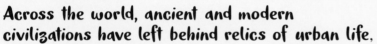

The stones of Machu Picchu were precisely cut, fitting perfectly together without the need for mortar.

MACHU PICCHU, PERU

Concealed high in the Andes Mountains in Peru, the city of Machu Picchu was built by the Incas in the 1400s. A masterpiece of engineering, its walls are constructed from hand-carved stones. The city was abandoned in the 1500s when the Spanish invaded and was then forgotten about by all but locals until the early 1900s, when it was "rediscovered" by Western explorers. Today Machu Picchu draws visitors from around the world who come to admire the ancient farms, houses, and temples.

POMPEII, ITALY

Pompeii was a thriving city in the ancient Roman Empire until it was buried by ash and rock from the eruption of the nearby volcano, Mount Vesuvius, in A.D. 79. The catastrophe that killed many hundreds of Pompeiians also perfectly preserved the city for thousands of years, allowing archaeologists to uncover a perfect snapshot of Roman life. Everything from food to furniture and even what people had in their pockets remained undisturbed under layers of rock.

Many of the city's clocks are frozen at 11:55—the moment the power went out.

PRIPYAT, UKRAINE

Built in 1970 to serve the nearby Chernobyl nuclear power plant, this city of around 50,000 people was evacuated in April 1986 when Chernobyl's reactor went into meltdown, contaminating the land nearby with deadly levels of radioactivity. Today the city remains largely as it was on the day it was abandoned, with toys left out in the schoolyard and classrooms still set up for lessons. Although radioactivity remains dangerously high in the surrounding 1,000 sq. mi. (2,600 km²) "Zone of Alienation," it has become an unexpected haven for wildlife in the absence of humans.

Petra is carved into pink sandstone canyons, so it was nicknamed "The Rose City."

TIANDUCHENG, CHINA

A recreation of Paris's architecture, this Chinese city features a replica of the Eiffel Tower, grand boulevards, and classical fountains modeled on the Palace of Versailles. Built in 2007 to house 10,000 people, it's one of many new cities intended to provide homes for China's rapidly growing population. But few residents have chosen to move here—and the district remains largely unoccupied.

PETRA, JORDAN

Petra was an ancient settlement constructed 2,500 years ago. It was an important hub for trade routes across the scorching deserts of the Middle East and is famous for its clever water supply, which used channels carved into its rock canyons to deliver enough water to support its people. When these channels were damaged in an earthquake and trading routes began moving from land to sea, Petra became less important, and it was abandoned in the 1200s.

MIGRATION IN KRAKÓW

A city's population changes over time, as people come and go, bringing different ideas, foods, languages, and customs with them. Migration such as this has had a great impact on the Polish city of Kraków. Changes brought on by trade, education, religion, and the violent shadow of war have transformed the identity of the city and the people who live there.

THE HEART OF KRAKÓW

As big as four football fields, Rynek Główny is one of Europe's largest and oldest town squares. Traders and travelers from across the continent have been drawn here for 750 years, and it remains the beating heart of the city today.

KRAKÓW

A war in 1795 wiped Poland off the map for 123 years, splitting its land between Russia, Austria, and Prussia. Kraków became an independent city-state that attracted many new migrants. Many of them were Polish, seeking their lost national identity. The country of Poland was restored in 1918, after World War I.

Kraków had a thriving Jewish community until 1939, when invading German Nazis began persecuting Jews. A few escaped to other countries, but only 1 in 10 Jewish Cracovians survived WWII. After the war, more prejudice against Jewish people forced most Jewish survivors to leave Kraków and build lives elsewhere.

About one-fourth of Kraków's residents are students, many of whom moved here to study.

Around 1 in 10 Cracovians come from outside Poland.

Immigrants arrive from another country. Emigrants leave to live somewhere else.

The Hejnał trumpet call is played hourly from St. Mary's Basilica by firefighters, who use the tower as a lookout.

Legend has it that Kraków was named after a young shoemaker named Krak, who tricked a dragon terrorizing the city into blowing itself up. "Kraków" means "Krak's City."

KRAKÓW STATS:
- Location: Poland, Europe
- Population: 770,000
- Language: Polish
- Residents are known as Cracovians
- Kraków's nickname is "The City of Churches"

KRAKÓW

In 2004, Poland joined the European Union—a group of countries who agree to share laws and allow free travel across their borders. Two million Polish people have since emigrated to other EU countries, seeking new opportunities.

RECENT MIGRATION

Six million people fled Ukraine when the country was invaded by Russia in 2022. A quarter of these people crossed the border to Poland, and many of them passed through Kraków on their journey to find safety elsewhere in Europe.

At Kraków's Główny train station, a 24-hour help desk offered support to refugees arriving from Ukraine.

Refugees are people who have been forced to leave their country because it's not safe to stay. Migrants move to a different country for other reasons—often to seek a better life.

Free information points across Kraków helped Ukrainian refugees find shelter, jobs, doctor appointments, and legal help.

PKP KRAKÓW GŁÓWNY

Over 6,000 refugee children have enrolled in Kraków's schools since the war in Ukraine began in 2022.

Public transportation is free for refugees in Kraków.

KRAKÓW

SNOW IN MONTREAL

Twelve million cubic metres of snow fall on this Canadian city each winter, which often don't melt for months. To prevent the weather paralysing its roads, railways, and cycle paths, an epic city-wide operation clears the snow into enormous storage mountains, which can be up to seven storeys high.

STORING SNOW

Montreal's snow is transported to 29 snow dumping sites around the city. Some sites are huge: the same size as 18 football fields!

The stone that built Montreal was dug out of the Francon Quarry. Now this quarry is the city's largest snow-dumping site, with 170 million cu. ft. (4.8 million m³) of snow delivered here each year.

Montreal is an island: it's the largest of more than 200 that make up the Hochelaga Archipelago.

A fourth of the city's snow is dumped into the sewer, where it is melted by waste water from houses.

In the winter, there are more than 125 mi. (200km) of cross-country ski trails through the city.

Montreal has 217 mi. (350 km) of bike paths.

Ice hockey was invented in Montreal. It's one of Canada's national sports.

It snows for around 60 days a year in Montreal. The record for snowfall was 18 in. (46 cm) in one day.

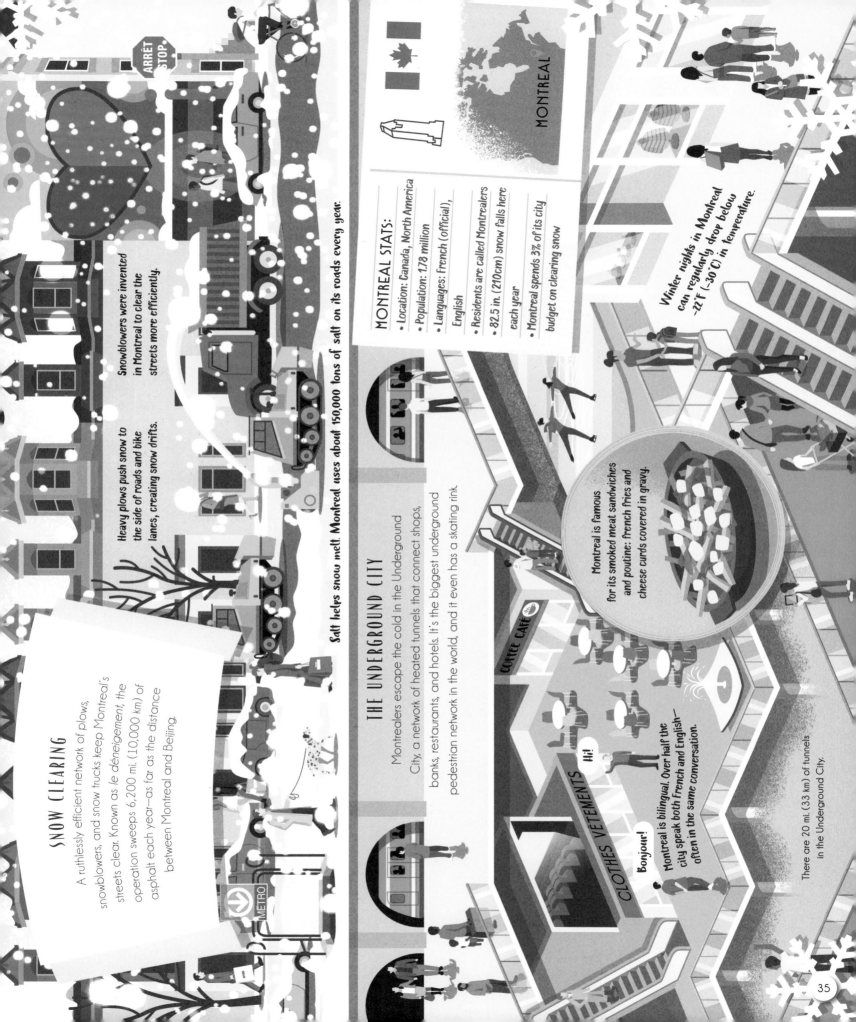

SNOW CLEARING

A ruthlessly efficient network of plows, snowblowers, and snow trucks keep Montreal's streets clear. Known as *le déneigement*, the operation sweeps 6,200 mi. (10,000 km) of asphalt each year—as far as the distance between Montreal and Beijing.

Snowblowers were invented in Montreal to clear the streets more efficiently.

Heavy plows push snow to the side of roads and bike lanes, creating snow drifts.

Salt helps snow melt. Montreal uses about 150,000 tons of salt on its roads every year.

ARRÊT STOP.

MÉTRO

THE UNDERGROUND CITY

Montrealers escape the cold in the Underground City, a network of heated tunnels that connect shops, banks, restaurants, and hotels. It's the biggest underground pedestrian network in the world, and it even has a skating rink.

There are 20 mi. (33 km) of tunnels in the Underground City.

CLOTHES VÊTEMENTS

Bonjour!

Hi!

Montreal is bilingual. Over half the city speak both French and English—often in the same conversation.

COFFEE CAFÉ

Montreal is famous for its smoked meat sandwiches and poutine: french fries and cheese curds covered in gravy.

MONTREAL STATS:

- **Location:** Canada, North America
- **Population:** 1.78 million
- **Languages:** French (official), English
- **Residents are called** Montrealers
- **82.5 in. (210cm) snow falls here each year**
- **Montreal spends 3% of its city budget on clearing snow**

MONTREAL

Winter nights in Montreal can regularly drop below -22°F (-30°C) in temperature.

35

FAITH IN MECCA

Places of worship have always been central to how cities are built. None are more so than in Mecca, home of Masjid Al-Haram, also known as the Great Mosque, the most holy site in the Muslim faith. The Great Mosque attracts three million pilgrims every year, and most of them visit during the same ten-day period.

Expanding the Great Mosque has cost around $100 billion, which makes it the world's most expensive building.

THE HAJJ
Traditionally, every Muslim must travel to Mecca once in their lifetime, in a pilgrimage known as the Hajj. Only Muslims are allowed in Mecca, and the Hajj takes place during Dhul Hijjah, the last month of the Islamic calendar.

Mecca is the focal point of Islam. Muslims pray in its direction five times a day, wherever they are on the globe.

At the center of the Mosque is the Kaaba, a holy shrine that Muslims consider to be the most sacred spot in the world.

THE GREAT MOSQUE
The Great Mosque is the largest mosque in the world, and the center of the Hajj. It is 1,400 years old, covers 1.4 sq. mi. (3.5 km²), and accommodates 2.5 million worshippers at once.

Over three million people visit for the Hajj each year. The Hajj is the world's largest human gathering.

The world's largest clock tower looks down on the Great Mosque, with faces up to 140 ft. (43m) wide.

MECCA

This seven-tower hotel and shopping complex houses pilgrims during the Hajj.

In the mosque, everyone wears the appropriate clothing, no matter their position in life. Comfortable, slip-on shoes are advised.

Pilgrims spend time visiting various holy sites around Mecca and the Great Mosque. The city has gone to great lengths to safely accommodate the huge crowds of worshippers.

Temperatures can reach 113°F (45°C) in Mina. Today's tents are air-conditioned, and pilgrims are given free cold water to help them avoid heatstroke.

There are separate tents for men and women.

Meccans consider their visitors "guests of god." They often give out cold water and free meals of rice and chicken to long lines of grateful pilgrims.

Each tent is fireproof and equipped with sprinklers and emergency exits.

EXIT

The Hajj brings people of many backgrounds and nationalities together from across the Muslim faith.

Mecca's metro runs for just 7 days a year during the Hajj, when it becomes the busiest line in the world. Trains carry 3,000 passengers and leave every two and a half minutes.

THE TENT CITY OF MINA

The valley of Mina near Mecca holds a huge city of 100,000 tents, where up to 2.6 million pilgrims can stay during the Hajj. For the other 51 weeks of the year the tents remain, but Mina is largely deserted.

GEOTHERMAL ENERGY IN
REYKJAVÍK

The colorful Northern Lights dance in Iceland's winter sky. Known as the "aurora borealis," they're made by tiny particles from space colliding in Earth's atmosphere.

Perched on a volcanic island in the chilly North Atlantic Ocean, Reykjavík survives its bitter winters by drawing heat and electricity from the earth itself. Among bubbling lava flows and hot springs, modern geothermal power plants generate clean and clever solutions to the thriving city's energy needs.

From December to January, Reykjavík has only five hours of sunlight a day. Between May and July, it's always light, as the sun never dips far beneath the horizon.

When magma erupts from a volcano, it's called lava. Flowing lava cools into solid rock, changing the shape of the land.

Most homes in Reykjavík don't need boilers to heat their water. Instead, hot water from geothermal power plants is piped to them directly.

VOLCANIC HEAT
Our planet's core is hot enough to melt rocks. Iceland sits on a gap in Earth's outer layer, the crust. When superheated liquid rock, called magma, oozes up to the crust, it causes volcanic activity.

REYKJAVÍK STATS:

- Location: Iceland, Europe
- Population: 140,000
- Language: Icelandic
- Residents are called Reykjavíkians
- Reykjavík is the world's most northerly capital city
- Iceland is Europe's most westerly country

REYKJAVÍK

Natural hot springs can reach temperatures of 104°F (40°C). They're full of minerals that are said to be great for the skin and health of bathers.

Rainwater falls into underground reservoirs, which are heated by magma. The water then bubbles up to the surface, forming hot springs.

Geysers are a type of natural hot spring, where heated water sometimes erupts into the air.

There are 32 active volcanoes in Iceland.

Iceland's national dish is Hákarl, which is fermented shark.

EARTH POWERED

Geothermal power plants make electricity using the heat of Earth's crust. Water is pushed down boreholes 1.9 mi. (3 km) deep. It returns as superheated steam, which turns turbines to generate power.

Geothermal means "Earth-heated."

Sulfur dioxide from Earth's crust makes geothermal hot water smell a bit like rotten eggs. Icelanders are used to it!

Geothermal water heats greenhouses, letting chilly Iceland grow plenty of fresh fruit, vegetables, and flowers.

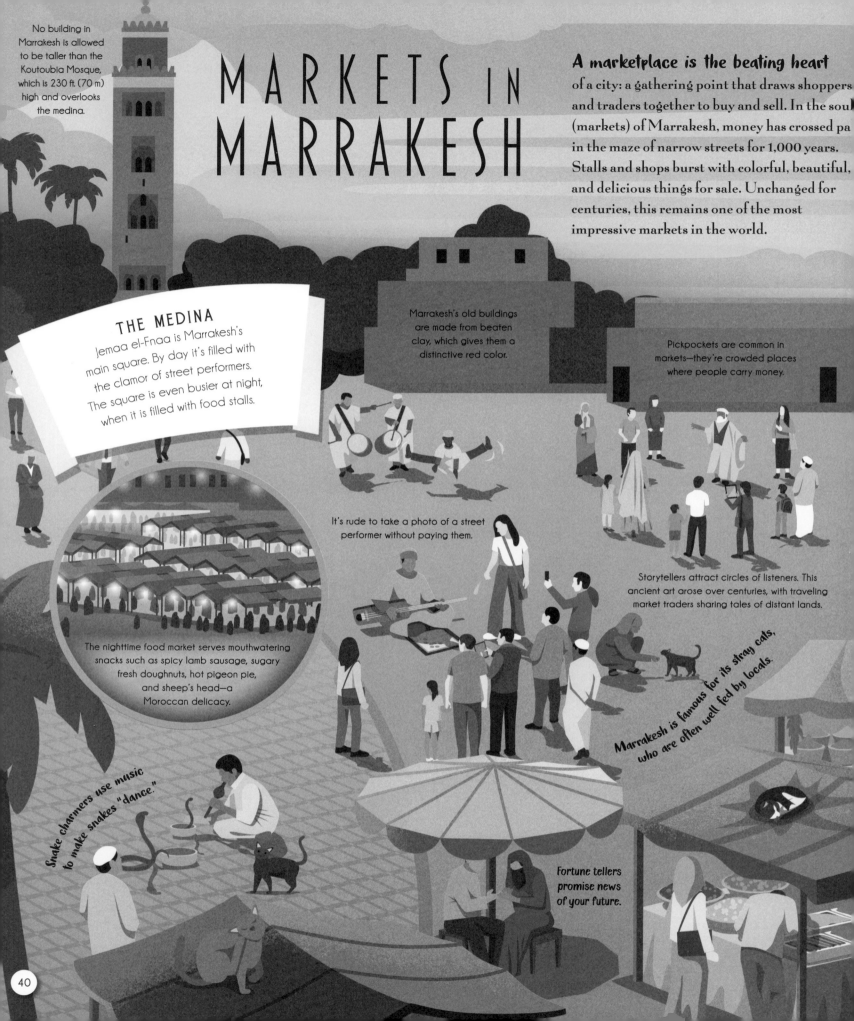

No building in Marrakesh is allowed to be taller than the Koutoubia Mosque, which is 230 ft. (70 m) high and overlooks the medina.

MARKETS IN MARRAKESH

A marketplace is the beating heart of a city: a gathering point that draws shoppers and traders together to buy and sell. In the soul (markets) of Marrakesh, money has crossed pa in the maze of narrow streets for 1,000 years. Stalls and shops burst with colorful, beautiful, and delicious things for sale. Unchanged for centuries, this remains one of the most impressive markets in the world.

THE MEDINA
Jemaa el-Fnaa is Marrakesh's main square. By day it's filled with the clamor of street performers. The square is even busier at night, when it is filled with food stalls.

Marrakesh's old buildings are made from beaten clay, which gives them a distinctive red color.

Pickpockets are common in markets—they're crowded places where people carry money.

It's rude to take a photo of a street performer without paying them.

Storytellers attract circles of listeners. This ancient art arose over centuries, with traveling market traders sharing tales of distant lands.

The nighttime food market serves mouthwatering snacks such as spicy lamb sausage, sugary fresh doughnuts, hot pigeon pie, and sheep's head—a Moroccan delicacy.

Marrakesh is famous for its stray cats, who are often well fed by locals.

Snake charmers use music to make snakes "dance."

Fortune tellers promise news of your future.

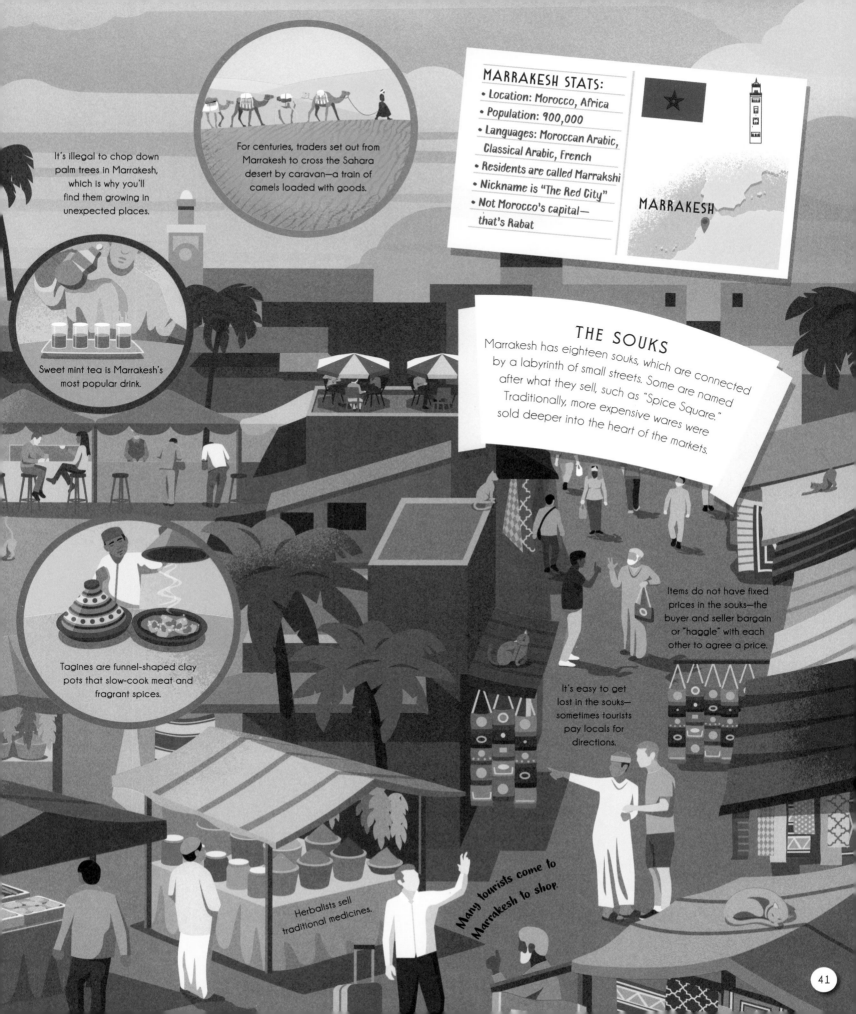

It's illegal to chop down palm trees in Marrakesh, which is why you'll find them growing in unexpected places.

For centuries, traders set out from Marrakesh to cross the Sahara desert by caravan—a train of camels loaded with goods.

MARRAKESH STATS:
• Location: Morocco, Africa
• Population: 900,000
• Languages: Moroccan Arabic, Classical Arabic, French
• Residents are called Marrakshi
• Nickname is "The Red City"
• Not Morocco's capital—that's Rabat

MARRAKESH

Sweet mint tea is Marrakesh's most popular drink.

THE SOUKS

Marrakesh has eighteen souks, which are connected by a labyrinth of small streets. Some are named after what they sell, such as "Spice Square." Traditionally, more expensive wares were sold deeper into the heart of the markets.

Tagines are funnel-shaped clay pots that slow-cook meat and fragrant spices.

Items do not have fixed prices in the souks—the buyer and seller bargain or "haggle" with each other to agree a price.

It's easy to get lost in the souks—sometimes tourists pay locals for directions.

Herbalists sell traditional medicines.

Many tourists come to Marrakesh to shop.

DISASTERS

Without careful planning, the forces of nature can overwhelm a city, with devastating results. Some of the world's greatest settlements have suffered through unexpected catastrophes, leading modern cities to adapt and become more resistant to disasters.

Shielded gutters prevent dry leaves from building up. They can catch fire easily.

"Fire breaks" are spaces between buildings or forests, designed to be too wide for fire to cross.

FIRE

Fires can burn cities to the ground: The Great Chicago Fire of 1871 lasted three days and destroyed a third of the city. Today's buildings are designed to resist fire, but it is still a risk, especially in hot, dry environments. Careful plans are made to stop fires from taking hold.

Evacuation routes are vital for cities at risk of fire, as traffic jams can be deadly.

EARTHQUAKES

Cities built near faultlines in the Earth's crust are vulnerable to earthquakes, which can shake buildings until they collapse. Quakes can also rupture power lines and gas pipes, which can cause fires and blackouts and cut off the water supply. Modern cities use clever technology to adapt to earthquakes.

Torre Reforma in Mexico City has deep foundations and is designed to bend during earthquakes.

Taipei 101, a 1,640 ft. (500 m) tall skyscraper, has a 730-ton steel pendulum inside it to absorb shaking from quakes and high winds.

The Transamerica Pyramid in San Francisco has a base wider than its tip, to make it stable.

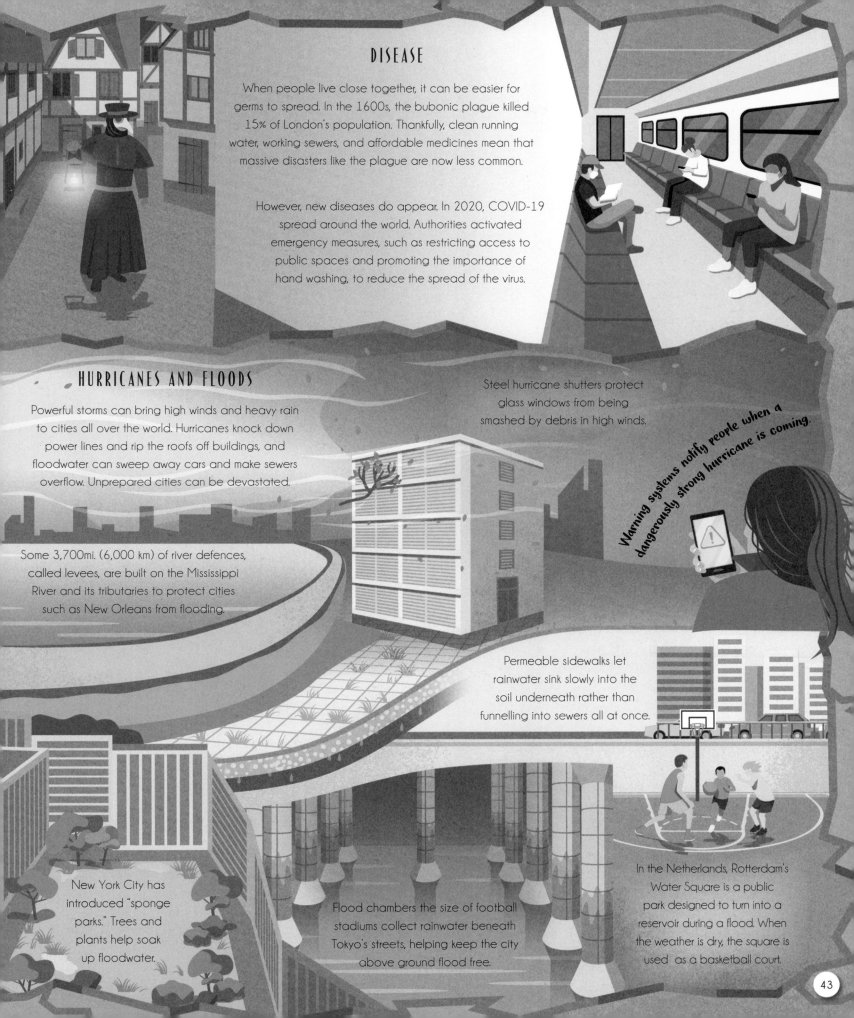

DISEASE

When people live close together, it can be easier for germs to spread. In the 1600s, the bubonic plague killed 15% of London's population. Thankfully, clean running water, working sewers, and affordable medicines mean that massive disasters like the plague are now less common.

However, new diseases do appear. In 2020, COVID-19 spread around the world. Authorities activated emergency measures, such as restricting access to public spaces and promoting the importance of hand washing, to reduce the spread of the virus.

HURRICANES AND FLOODS

Powerful storms can bring high winds and heavy rain to cities all over the world. Hurricanes knock down power lines and rip the roofs off buildings, and floodwater can sweep away cars and make sewers overflow. Unprepared cities can be devastated.

Some 3,700mi. (6,000 km) of river defences, called levees, are built on the Mississippi River and its tributaries to protect cities such as New Orleans from flooding.

Steel hurricane shutters protect glass windows from being smashed by debris in high winds.

Warning systems notify people when a dangerously strong hurricane is coming.

Permeable sidewalks let rainwater sink slowly into the soil underneath rather than funnelling into sewers all at once.

New York City has introduced "sponge parks." Trees and plants help soak up floodwater.

Flood chambers the size of football stadiums collect rainwater beneath Tokyo's streets, helping keep the city above ground flood free.

In the Netherlands, Rotterdam's Water Square is a public park designed to turn into a reservoir during a flood. When the weather is dry, the square is used as a basketball court.

AIR POLLUTION

Air pollution is caused by toxic gases and microscopic dust called particulates, which are usually from vehicles, factories, and anything that burns fossil fuels. China has grown quickly since the 1970s, building many new cities and more roads and railroads. This has caused even more pollution, especially in big cities such as Beijing. Breathing polluted air every day can make us ill.

CLEAN AIR IN BEIJING

Busy Beijing is the capital of China, the world's second most populated country. Like many big cities, Beijing has struggled with air pollution. It was once prone to "airpocalypses," which made it dangerous to breathe outside. However, the people of Beijing have worked hard to clean up the air, using clever schemes to shrink pollution even while the city grows.

CITY LIFE

People used to live in traditional siheyuans—courtyard houses—with colorful hutongs (alleys) between them. As the population has increased, most people now live in huge, modern tower buildings, which fit more people inside.

Crispy roast duck is a popular dish in Beijing. It is eaten in pancakes, with rich hoisin sauce.

Air pollution creates a layer of smog (smoke and fog), which makes it difficult to see. Smog can make it dangerous to drive, fly, or even be outside. On some days it can even block out sunlight.

Beijing's Weather Modification Office uses rockets and planes to fire chemicals into the sky to make it rain. This can reduce pollution from dust storms and clear smog. It's also been used to make it snow on national holidays.

China is investing in "clean" energy, such as wind and solar power.

BEIJING STATS:
- Location: China, Asia
- Population: 22 million
- Languages: Mandarin
- Residents are called Beijingers
- The city is 3,000 years old
- Beijing has seven UNESCO World Heritage Sites

BEIJING

Gasoline and diesel cars are prohibited from driving in Beijing on certain days of the week. Electric cars can drive every day.

China has 99% of the world's electric buses.

Tai chi is an ancient Chinese martial art. Its gentle movements are often practiced in Beijing parks.

GREEN TECHNOLOGY
A popular app gives people points for making green choices, such as taking public transportation. These points allow them to plant real trees. Pollution sensors around the city mean that anyone can check the air quality on their phone. They also alert police to polluters.

Go, or "wei-ch'i," is the world's oldest board game. It has been played in China for around 4,000 years.

Trees help reduce air pollution. Every Chinese citizen age 11 and up is encouraged to plant at least three trees every year.

CABLE CARS IN MEDELLÍN

Nestled among cloud-capped mountains in Colombia. Medellín's steep and twisting roads make traveling through the city a headache. To help, a system of cable cars, known as the "Metrocable," was built in 2004. It sweeps passengers over rooftops in style and has linked the far-flung corners of this sprawling metropolis together for the first time.

MEDELLÍN STATS:

- Location: Colombia, South America
- Population: 2.5 million
- Language: Spanish
- Residents from this part of Colombia are called Paisas
- The first city in the world to use cable cars for mass transit

MEDELLÍN

CONNECTING THE CITY

A sprawling mountain city, Medellín has 249 barrios (neighborhoods). Its center is 5,000 ft. (1,500 m) above sea level, and its hillsides reach up to 0.6 mi. (1 km) higher. Each cable car line lifts or lowers passengers about 980 ft. (300 m), sometimes passing through the clouds.

There used to be almost no public spaces in Medellín. It now hopes to have 160 sq. ft. (15 m²) of public space per person by 2030.

Library parks have opened in poorer barrios, creating spaces for residents to socialize, play, study, and celebrate.

Isolated from the city, it was hard for residents in the mountain barrios to find work, and it was easy for criminals to thrive. Linking these barrios to the rest of Medellín has made them safer and more prosperous.

With no motor in a car, the ride is almost silent, unlike buses or trains.

Medellín's six cable car lines can carry up to 4,000 people per hour in each direction.

46

THE METROCABLE MIRACLE

By integrating poorer and richer neighborhoods, Metrocable has helped forge a new identity for Medellín, transforming it from one of the world's most violent places into a global cultural hotspot.

Colombia is the biggest grower of flowers in the southern hemisphere.

Medellín's metro trains can't climb the steep slopes at the city's edge.

The narrow, winding hillside roads take hours to navigate by bus. By cable car, the journey takes minutes.

Outdoor escalators help residents climb very steep hills.

Medellín is famous for its art, music, and culture. Its colorful street art murals draw crowds from around the world.

Medellín is known as the "city of the eternal spring" because its constant temperature means flowers are in bloom all year round.

Guarapo—sugar cane juice—is sweet and refreshing.

Corn bread pancakes called *arepas* are eaten with almost every meal, often stuffed with ground meat, rice, avocado, eggs, red beans, plantain, and onion sauce.

ATHENS STATS:
- Location: Greece, Europe
- Population: 3 million
- Language: Greek
- Residents are called Athenians
- One of the world's oldest constantly inhabited cities

ATHENS

Athena's favorite animal, the owl, is the city's symbol.

THE ANCIENT CITY

Athens is named after the Greek goddess of wisdom, Athena. Legend has it she and Poseidon, god of the sea, each gave gifts to the city. Athena's—an olive tree—was judged the winner over Poseidon's fountain of salt water.

The Acropolis is a cluster of ancient buildings on a rocky outcrop in the heart of Athens.

An olive tree that grows in the Acropolis is said to be "Athena's Tree."

The Parthenon was once a temple to the goddess Athena. Over its 2,500-year history it has been a church, a mosque, and an ammunition storage site. Today it is preserved as a heritage site.

Olives are a symbol of peace and have been prized in Greece for over 5,000 years.

Democracy is a way people can choose their governments and laws by voting. It was invented in ancient Athens.

Theater was invented in Athens as a way of celebrating Dionysus, the Greek god of pleasure. Early performances told stories of the gods, watched by thousands in huge amphitheaters, which were cut into rock.

Modern Athens has more theaters than any other city.

The Greek capital of Athens is one of the oldest cities in the world. The source of much of Western art, government, and philosophy, it was fought over by armies and empires for millennia. Today Athens is a showcase of thousands of years of history, where commuter trains rattle past ancient monuments, and archaeologists find hidden treasures in the foundations of rising skyscrapers.

HISTORY IN ATHENS

4,000 years of architecture can be found in Athens's streets.

OLYMPIC GAMES
Created by the ancient Greeks in 776 B.C., the Olympic Games were held in Athens in summer 2004. New stadiums, streetcars, housing, and hotels were rapidly built, transforming parts of the ancient city and making the games a big success.

Today many parts of the Olympics' new infrastructure lie abandoned, as modern ruins.

There isn't room to display every artifact found in Athens, so most are kept in storage.

Ancient ruins are everywhere in Athens— preserved in the cellars of popular stores, the foyers of hotels, and the storerooms of factories.

"Rescue excavations" are a legal requirement on construction sites to check for ancient artifacts, with some guarded by police against thieves.

Smartphone apps let visitors see where ancient buildings and city walls once stood.

Syntagma Square Metro station is built through an ancient necropolis (a burial place for the dead). Commuters walk alongside preserved artifacts and tombs as they alight from trains and make their way to the city's modern parliament building above.

TECHNOLOGY IN SEOUL

Technology is a way of life in the city of Seoul, where electronics and superfast Internet mean almost anything can be done digitally. With 24-hour gaming cafés, state of the art smart homes, automatic transportation, and even robot waiters, this is one of the most forward-thinking cities in the world.

24-HOUR CITY
Seoul has an around-the-clock culture, which means that restaurants, gaming cafés, public baths, and convenience stores are open all day and all night.

About 20% of South Korea's wealth comes from Samsung, the country's global tech giant.

Smart homes are common in Seoul. Heat, doors, stoves, and even beds are powered by apps and AI.

Seoul has thousands of cafés, and many of them have themes, such as "teddy bears" or "a rainy day." Some of them let guests mingle with animals, including cats, dogs, and even sheep!

There are over 10,000 karaoke bars in Seoul.

Some buses in Seoul are driverless.

고양이 카페

고양이

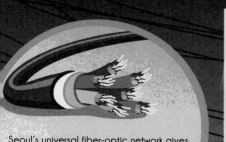

Seoul's universal fiber-optic network gives it one of the fastest Internet speeds in the world. Fiber-optic cables send data through strands of woven glass at the speed of light.

Baseball is the most popular sport in South Korea.

SEOUL

PC BANGS

PC bangs are popular Internet cafés with ultrafast and powerful terminals, where gamers can gather to eat, drink, and play video games with friends.

ESports—competitive online gaming—is hugely popular in Seoul and has its own stadiums.

Robot waiters serve food in some restaurants. You may also be able to order via touchscreen.

Seoul has almost 5,000 PC bangs.

피시방

South Korea opened the world's first Internet addiction camp to help teenagers "detox" from too much time online.

김치

레스토랑

음식과 음료

식품 시장

Side dishes called "banchan," such as kimchi or beansprouts, are usually refilled free of charge, as Koreans value treating guests generously.

Night markets serve yummy street food such as tteok-bokki, which are stick-shaped, flavored rice cakes.

CYCLING IN COPENHAGEN

Denmark's capital city has been building bike paths for over a hundred years, and it now boasts one of the most extensive cycling networks in the world. Replacing cars and vans with bikes makes Copenhagen's streets cleaner, safer, and quieter. A clever bike-friendly design throughout the city means that cycling is usually the fastest, cheapest, and healthiest way to travel.

BIKE-FRIENDLY

More people choose to ride bikes when their city makes it easy for them. Copenhagen's wide and plentiful bicycle lanes make it safe and enjoyable to travel around by bike.

Almost all mail in Copenhagen is delivered by bicycle.

Many taxis in Copenhagen have bike racks on the back.

Conversation lanes are wide enough for riders to chat.

Air pumps on the street help riders fix flat tires.

Copenhagen has more bikes than people!

Traffic lights allow cyclists to pass before cars.

BIKES FIRST

During rush hour, traffic lights are timed in a "green wave" so that riders on the busiest routes never need to stop. Special signals help cyclists time their ride so they reach the lights at the right time.

About 10 bikes fit into the space of one car. But with cycling so popular in Copenhagen, it can be difficult finding a place to park your bike.

Suburban trains have a car just for bikes.

Public stairways have ramps to make it easier to push bikes up them.

Cargo bikes can be adapted into many things, including portable shops.

Trash cans are angled so cyclists can throw refuse in while riding past.

Copenhagen is surrounded by water and is famous for its fish, especially pickled herring.

Around half of Copenhageners travel to work or school by bike.

Most children learn to ride bikes before they start school.

Riders can rest on special railings at traffic lights.

The cargo bike was invented in Copenhagen.

COPENHAGEN STATS:
- Location: Denmark, Europe
- Population: 600,000
- Language: Danish
- Residents are called Copenhageners
- Copenhagen is often ranked the world's best city for a riding bike

COPENHAGEN

WILDLIFE

Cities are designed for humans, but they're often home to many other creatures. Sometimes new buildings encroach on habitats, forcing wildlife to adapt to new environments, and sometimes animals are drawn to the quirks of a city. Around the world, beasts large and small make their homes in cities—with each embracing the wildlife in its own unique way.

MONKEYS IN NEW DELHI

Mischievous monkeys wreak havoc in India's capital city, breaking into houses, stealing food, and causing chaos in traffic. The monkeys are scared away from busy places using posters of langurs, their predator, and people hired to mimic the langur's shriek.

DEER IN NARA

Tame deer roam freely in the Japanese city of Nara. Protected by law, the deer have learned to bow to humans in exchange for treats—and snack vendors sell special "deer crackers" to feed them.

鹿の餌

BLACK BEARS IN ASHEVILLE

In North Carolina, black bears often emerge from nearby forests to prowl suburban streets, digging through garbage cans and even playing in backyards. Some are even seen padding past shops downtown, where they're escorted back home by police.

STOCKHOLM SUBWAY SPIDER

Kungsträdgården station on the Stockholm metro is home to the rare *Lessertia dentichelis* spider, which isn't found anywhere else in Sweden. Scientists suspect that the spiders arrived on foreign tunneling equipment used to dig the station, but nobody is quite sure.

PELICANS IN LONDON

Pelicans have made their home in St. James's Park since a pair were given to King Charles II in the 1600s. Today these sociable birds catch fish from the lake and are usually seen basking in the sun on their favorite rocks.

WILD BOARS IN BERLIN

About 5,000 of Germany's native wild boars live in Berlin, where 20% of the land is green space. They're most visible in the spring, when they raise their piglets, often in people's flowerbeds and front yards.

PYTHONS IN BANGKOK

The reticulated python is the world's longest snake and a common sight in Bangkok, Thailand, where the city's pest hotline gets a call about a snake every fifteen minutes. Pythons thrive in the city's wetlands but have now taken to the sewers, sometimes climbing into people's houses through their toilet.

POSSUMS IN SYDNEY

Used to living in tree hollows, brushtail possums have adapted to city life by making homes in the roofs of houses. These nocturnal animals scamper around by night, feasting on plants and vegetables. However, their numbers are dwindling because of loss of habitat, urban predators, and traffic.

BATS IN AUSTIN

One and a half million bats live under a bridge in downtown Austin, Texas, erupting into the sky at sunset. These nocturnal animals are common sights in many cities, roosting in quiet dark spots like roof cavities and foraging for food in parks, ponds, and gardens.

DOGS IN MOSCOW

Stray dogs are widespread in Moscow and can be seen crossing streets with pedestrians, obeying traffic lights, and even making regular trips on the city's metro. The dogs move in packs and have a variety of strategies to get food from locals.

WATER IN ISTANBUL

From Roman aqueducts to Victorian plumbing, we've always had to find unique ways to keep the faucets running. Underneath Istanbul is a network of cisterns (water tanks) the size of cathedrals. They kept this ancient capital of the Ottoman Empire supplied with water for a millennium.

The Valens aqueduct was built by the Romans to supply the city with water.

Istanbul's aqueduct system was the largest in the ancient world, at over 155 mi. (250 km) long.

In Roman times, water reached Istanbul's cisterns via aqueducts: a network of underground water channels, pipes, tunnels, and bridges that carried the water from reservoirs more than 125 mi. (200 km) away.

Reservoirs can be made by damming rivers.

BASILICA CISTERN

The Basilica Cistern is the largest in Istanbul. It is about 450 ft. (140 m) long and 200 ft. (60 m) wide, and can hold about 160 swimming pools' worth of water. It was forgotten for centuries, until people discovered they could fish through holes in their cellar floors.

Cisterns are a way of storing clean water underground so it can be used later. Several hundred ancient cisterns lie below Istanbul's streets, but nobody knows the exact number.

The cistern's 300 stone columns were salvaged from ancient temples.

People throw coins into the cistern for good luck.

Carp live in the ancient cistern.

TWO CONTINENTS

Istanbul is the only city in the world that spans two continents. Its European and Asian sides are separated by the Bosphorus, a narrow strait of water.

ISTANBUL STATS:

- Location: Turkey, Europe/Asia
- Population: 15 million
- Language: Turkish
- Residents are called Istanbulites
- This city was the capital of three ancient empires: Rome, Ottoman, Byzantium
- Istanbul is Turkey's largest city, but Ankara is the capital

ISTANBUL

A tunnel under the Bosphorus pumps fresh water from reservoirs on the Asian side of the city to the European side.

The Bosphorus is a busy shipping lane.

MODERN PLUMBING

All water comes from nature: rain fills up rivers and reservoirs and stocks up underground supplies. Modern Istanbul uses pumps and pipes to move water but still collects it from reservoirs and dams in the same way the Romans did.

There are more than 3,000 mosques in Istanbul.

Praying for rain is a common ritual in Turkey. "Yağmur duası," the rain prayer, involves blessing 7,000 small stones and carrying them to the top of a hill.

Around 125,000 stray cats live in Istanbul. Communal cat houses and vending machines provide them with shelter, food, and water.

Modern cities can get their water from the ground (using wells), from rainwater, or from rivers. They can also remove the salt from seawater, using a process called desalinization.

Today Istanbul's modern water pipe network is longer than Earth is wide.

PORTS IN ROTTERDAM

Straddling three rivers as they pour into the fierce North Sea, the Dutch city of Rotterdam is home to Europe's largest port. Here a sprawling web of cranes and ships process almost half a billion tons of cargo from around the world each year.

THE DOCK

About 80 ships arrive in Rotterdam every 24 hours, day and night. Up to 1,300 ft. (400 m) long, they carry food, coal, iron, oil, clothes, microchips, and more. Your copy of this book is likely to have traveled through the dock here.

Container ships are timetabled, like buses. To ship something, a company will buy space in a container and arrange their cargo's transportation to and from the boat.

Smaller ships can carry cargo inland on rivers and canals.

Ships can moor up using buoys in the water, so cargo can be transferred between vessels.

Shipping is the most energy-efficient way to transport heavy cargo long distances. However, pollution from ships can harm our ocean's ecosystems, and their fuel releases greenhouse gases.

Oil refineries at the port convert crude oil from tanker ships into gasoline, diesel, and other useful chemicals. Pipelines carry these to other parts of Europe. Some is kept at the port to fuel ships.

Tugboats with powerful engines maneuver bigger ships around th

Rotterdam is famous for apple pie and stroopwafel—sweet caramel sandwiched between two thin waffles.

Robotic gantry cranes can be up to 150 ft. (46 m) high.

One of the port's five terminals is automated: robot cranes unload the ships without human help. It's nicknamed the "ghost terminal."

Driverless vehicles navigate the terminal by using an electromagnetic grid buried in the asphalt.

Standard shipping containers are always 8 ft. (2.4 m) wide, 8.5 ft. (2.6 m) high, and either 20 ft. (6 m) or 40 ft. (12 m) long.

About 1,300 containers are lost at sea every year.

JS1809

Every container in the world has a unique reference number on it so that it can be tracked.

SHIPPING CONTAINERS

Shipping containers are large metal boxes that are used to transport goods all over the world. They come in standard sizes, so that every port can use the same equipment to handle them. They can be loaded onto ships, trucks, and trains without needing to be opened and repacked.

12 million containers pass through Rotterdam every year.

Modern cargo ships can carry thousands of containers.

Rotterdam is a hub for different kinds of transportation, like ships, rail and road.

CARNIVAL IN RIO

The biggest party on Earth is held every year in Rio de Janeiro, where millions gather for the annual Carnival. A riotous five-day celebration of indulgence, color, and excess, Carnival transforms Rio into a gigantic street party where everyone is welcome. The celebrations are dominated by samba, an energetic dance forged in Rio's poorer neighborhoods.

SAMBADROMO

Carnival features a fierce contest among more than 100 samba schools in Rio, each hoping to be crowned the best. They perform elaborate choreographed parades in the Sambadromo (Sambadrome), a 2,300 ft. (700 m) long stadium. The top prize in the samba contest is millions of dollars, as well as intense local pride.

The extraordinary Carnival costumes can cost as much as $10,000 to make. Millions of beads are often sewn on by hand.

Samba was invented in the favelas (poor, overcrowded areas) by enslaved Africans and their descendants. The dance is a celebration and also an escape from a difficult life.

Samba dancers perform to rhythmic drum beats, and the crowd often dances along too!

PHANTOM RIVER

Rio de Janeiro is named after a river that doesn't exist: an explorer thought Rio's bay was the mouth of a river, naming it the "January River."

Rio's famous statue of Christ the Redeemer is over 98 ft. (30 m) tall. It's struck by lightning about three times a year.

A quarter of Rio's residents live in favelas. Most of its samba schools can be found here. Around 90,000 people watch the parade inside the Sambadromo.

Temperatures can reach 104°F (40°C) during Carnival.

BLOCOS

About 600 informal street parties, called "blocos," are held across the city during Carnival so that everyone can join the party. "Bandas" (street bands) play, and the blocos often have fun themes.

Parade floats can be the size of a building!

Thousands of designers, musicians, painters, and costumers work for months behind the scenes to prepare the parade and make their communities proud.

RIO STATS:
- Location: Brazil, South America
- Population: 6.7 million
- Language: Portuguese
- Residents are called Cariocas
- Two million people celebrate during each day of Carnival
- Carnival culminates in Mardi Gras—the day before Lent

RIO DE JANEIRO

PARKS IN SINGAPORE

As cities grow, nature is often swallowed by concrete and skyscrapers. However, green space is vital for a population's mental and physical health. Despite its densely packed population, 46% of the bustling city of Singapore is covered in greenery. Thanks to careful planning, every citizen has easy access to a public park.

Singapore is the world's third-densest country. Over 20,800 people live in each square mile (2.6 km²): 200 times as many as the U.S.

CITY IN A GARDEN
Greenery helps cool the city down, cleans the air, encourages wildlife, and makes people feel better by helping them reconnect with nature.

Singapore's aim is for everyone to live no more than 10 minutes from a park.

The National Parks Board gives out free seed packets to encourage Singaporeans to grow their own plants.

Chewing gum is banned in Singapore, and littering is punishable by a hefty fine or community service.

Singapore's pedestrians are the fastest walkers in the world, averaging over 3.7 mph (6 km/h).

Four large nature reserves help clean Singapore's air and water, and preserve its biodiversity. The Bukit Timah Reserve is said to have more species of trees than all of North America.

Nature playgrounds let children explore natural habitats through play. They're built from wood, stone, and plants.

GARDENS BY THE BAY
Gardens by the Bay is downtown Singapore's "green lung," a futuristic nature park twice the size of Disneyland.

The Flower Dome is the world's largest conservatory.

These human-made "Supertrees" are 164 ft. (50 m) high. Their concrete cores are covered in plants, solar panels, and rainwater collectors. At night, they light up and play music.

Singapore's emblem is a merlion.

OUR GREAT CITIES

Hopefully you've enjoyed traveling to some of the world's most magnificent cities, and discovering what makes them epic.

Every country thinks differently about what makes a city, and there's no one agreed definition. Each city is a living system: a network of pieces clicking together to make life work for the many people who live there.

Cities can be the roots of empires, and the engines of a nation's wealth—but they can also be crowded, smelly, and hot. To make life in a city fulfilling for everyone we must think carefully about what we build, and how we build it—now and for the future.

As the world's population continues to grow, more and more of us will be living in cities. New cities will appear, and the ones we know will get bigger and busier. We will need to get even better at living together.

Luckily, the world is full of amazing ideas about how we might build better lives for ourselves, and how we might turn to the past to solve the problems of the future.

What do you think about the place you live in? How has it changed over time, and what might happen to it next? What would you build there, and how would that affect other people, the wildlife, the traffic, and the quality of the air? How could you solve those problems? Clever ideas go a long way to making cities better for everyone. Even the smallest thing can have a big impact, such as tilted trash cans for cyclists in Copenhagen, heated subway seats in Tokyo, and a hotel for stray cats in Istanbul.

Cities are never finished. They are always changing, because we are always changing: apartment blocks rise up; a bridge stretches over a canal; old buildings become restaurants and hotels; an abandoned highway becomes a park. As we make our way into the future, we will shape our cities around us. There is no end to the possibilities we can imagine for ourselves.

Bon voyage!

About the author
Sam Sedgman is the award-winning author of the bestselling Adventures on Trains series, a confirmed nerd and an enthusiastic ferroequinologist. He lives in London, on top of a railroad station, and travels whenever he can.

About the illustrator
Daniel Long is a Norfolk-based illustrator with a love of exploring and nature. When not in his studio working he can be found exploring the local rivers and coast with his dog Hendrix.